WORLD ON FIRE

Fuelled By Faith

BY

THE PARTISIAN POET

1

'BIDEN BIDEN HE'S OUR MAN'

Biden, they said, he's our man if he can't do it, no one can.
Four years of riding the Biden Poseidon,
Four years of hiding, who auto-penned like a trident.
Through the murkiness and shadows, truth rises like a
diadem.
Media, which was slanting, is now recanting.
We did not know, we simply didn't see it's the inner circle
White House who hid it. We believed.
We are not to blame, we fell for the ruse, Oops, sorry about
that, we feel so obtuse.
Let's all move forward. I now have the sources to remedy
our errors you know we're remorseful.
Don't bring up the past, I was blinded by Biden.
I now have the details there's no more lying.
We're here to help, please believe all our crying.
The past is the past to the future we're implying.
We now know the truth, we're ready to go.
Let's forget those proclamations,
And move forward as a nation.

'DARKNESS TO LIGHT'

From the darkness,
What starkness the light can be.
The truth will always set you free.
When the shadows of the night block your sight,
It's time to change, time to stop.
There is only one way, one truth, one life.
There is only one that always shines bright,
Who left the heavens and the realm above
To walk amongst us and declare His love.
There is only one who healed the blind, sick, and lame.
You are the reason, the reason He came.
He holds you in His hand, He knows you by name.
The darkness comes when it seems there is no light.
There's strength in your weakness, your broken spirit is
contrite.
Uplift all your burdens to the one Majesty
The Son of the Father wants to make you family.
What a privilege it is to be a daughter, a son,
Of the Most High God, who is three in one.
What a day it is when
He finally makes you His.
He clears your debts, your flaws, and your sins.
Now is the moment. Now, don't wait.
Salvation is near, it is at the very gate.
He is waiting patiently for the door to your heart.
He is knocking today, His Spirit will impart
Conviction in righteousness, it's His part to play.
Sanctification: the process, come what may.
A continuous race where we stumble and trip,

Our faith is refined with a rod and a stick.
To chastise us with love, which comes from above,
Is proof enough when push comes to shove.
Light dispels the dark.

'JAGUAR CAUGHT BY THE JUGULAR'

Jaguar falling to the same selective,
Why would you take such a directive?
Such a proud history, and now lots of inventory.
I think you made a *mistaguar*,
And now in vague stage you are.
Supporting a pride agenda has left you in a sales dilemma.
Wow, 97 percent drop! What a slop in a marketing blender.
I think you should return to sender and amend your
advertising.
You should have learnt from the other brands diving.
Driving, it seems, into a brick wall.
Such a call, and now you befall,
The weight of your actions, causing factions.
Amongst your customers, who now run for the door.
They don't ask for more, you are left looking poor.
So don't ignore your customer base.
Apologize now, before it's too late.

'OFFICER TATUM ATTACKING YOUR CRANIUM'

Like an attack on your cranium,
An assertive conservative,
Who defends the narrative.
What is good and what is proper, he cuts like a lopper.
Through the blind leftist maze and the mists of their haze.
Once again with the facts and stats to match,
He leaves them stumbling, looking for a match.
He watches the madness, sometimes with sadness.
Forcing his hand, he stands up like a man.
Through his conviction is a depiction of strength.
He asks for your prayers because he doesn't relent.
He won't stop, he won't slow, just to let you know.
With merch and logos, slogans and clips,
He stands up and stands true and never flips.
Officer Tatum, a voice of reason in a world of treason.
I salute your character and your integrity.
I pray for your strength, your ministry, and your longevity.

'OLD MCMEDIA HAD A FARM'

Old McMedia had a farm, Ee I Ee I You,
And on that farm they created some harm,
With a lie here and a lie there,
Here a lie, there a lie, everywhere a lie-lie.
Old McMedia had a farm, Ee I Ee I You.
Old McMedia had a farm,
And on that farm there was a narrative,
With a drama here and a drama there,
Here a drama, there a drama, everywhere a drama-drama.
Old McMedia had a farm, Ee I Ee I You.
Old McMedia had a farm,
Ee I Ee I You,
And on that farm they had some liberals, Ee I Ee I You,
With a protest here, a protest there,
Here a protest, there a protest, everywhere a protest-protest.
Old McMedia had a farm, Ee I Ee I You.

'PHENTANOL IS BEING SOLD'

Phentanol, like methanol, is explosive and destructive.
Like power-consuming, the users are unproductive.
On the streets, on the screens, a zombie apocalypse is what
it seems.
Needles, like used-up matchsticks, are lying on the ground,
Contaminated people walking all around.
Diseased and defeated, what is the answer?
Spreading like wildfire, spreading like cancer.
The Judge on *The Five* said history has the proof,
Threaten them with jail time, put them all under one roof.
Riddled with tents, boxes, and bags,
It's easy to get despondent, it's easy to be sad.
A change is a-coming. We, the people, will decide.
Don't get off the roller coaster until it's the end of the ride.

'PICK UP YOUR CROSS'

Carry your cross, no matter the cost.
Follow me, or you'll remain lost.
In the darkness, He stays bright.
He carries my burdens and makes them light.
I fall and I fall, I keep those things, they are my plight.
Lord, please forgive me, You make me right.

Return to the fray, return to the fold.
Ask for forgiveness, then His Spirit will make you bold.
Turn from your sins, turn from those ways.
Let peace and love guard your days.

If I don't pick up my cross and keep on denying,
My life will be empty, and I will keep on lying.
I'll think life is good, life is purposeful,
But in reality, I am not fulfilled, it's His game, and I'm just
in it.

Bearing my cross and carrying the weight,
Can only be accepted when I'm called on by faith.
It is something worth hoping for, something unseen,
It's always where I'm going, not where I've been.

It's fixing my eyes on the Savior and tuning my behavior,
Being disciplined in all things to make myself stronger,
But always remembering the One I belong to.
Accepting my faults by seeking His grace,
And having His mercy in my life every day.

I bear my cross, but He carries me.
He leads me, He shadows me.

He's beside, He's in front, He never leaves me alone. So don't be afraid where you're at, come home, come home.

'TAPPER THE TRAPPER'

Yes, let's write a book.
Oh, what's the hook?
That Biden wasn't lying, because the Media was
complying, they were complicit in the cover up.
No, we never dressed it up.
Biden was never messed up.
He was as sharp as a tack.
The best version ever, he was right on track, really, really
clever, we heard them say.
He'll never fade, he'll never sway, like walking up the
stairs, exiting stage right, finding the right page.
I don't need a tell prompter, I can talk all night.
Oh, what a tangled web we weave, when the American
people we deceive.
And now a Tapper trapper of nightmare proportions, full of
confidants who witnessed the distortion.
People close to the inner circle, firsthand accounts, what a
lot of burble.
We were expected to believe what we saw was not real,
That the deception was so good, such a well devised shield,
That our eyes wide open shut,
That our ears were like what.
Surely, people will see through this open display, that
Tapper the trapper always saw this decay.
I have humility, I say to that bay, I'm prepared for the heat
to get my payday.
Still searching for prominence, still protesting innocence.
Tapper the trapper, we see through your display, we know
your unworthy, your part of the decay.

'NO POLICE'

Let's get rid of law and order.
Let's let them all cross the border.
Who cares who comes, who cares when?
Our country will go on, it will never end.
But are we honest, can we see the truth?
Can we deny what's in the mix, what's about to brew?
All this chaos, all this disorder, but yet you say our country
is clear, no ripples in the water.
No immorality, only identity, we are fighting for our rights:
past, present, and future.
We need reparation so that we can nurture
This generation of proud Americans,
Who will stand up for freedom and liberty, who will seek
the truth no matter what they see.
So who needs rules, who needs laws? Let's all get along
and celebrate our flaw.

'LITTLE JIM JORDAN'

Little Jim Jordan,
Said, "How's the border?"
Debating that Dems made raids.
He put in a subpoena that changed his demeanor,
And said, "When will this craziness end?"

'BURN AND BURN'

Burn the cities,
Burn them down.
Anger, frustration are all around.
The average person who has invested
Is now under pressure, they are being tested.
They have spent their lives living the dream,
To what they thought was liberty.
Now, through pain, through fire and destruction,
They have lost it all, there was no protection.
But hold tight, don't let it go, your dreams, your lives, it's
not all woe.
There is only one who will make it right: God Almighty,
He's the one who fights.
Revenge is His. He promises that.
So sit and hold tight, because He knows all your facts.

'JOE AND JILL'

Joe and Jill went up the hill to fetch the Presidency after.
Jill took the crown, when Joe was down and the media
came tumbling after.

'WAITING FOR JOE'

Joe Rogan, what a slogan for seekers of truth.
What a banner of cross-connection, from your fighting
background to a podcast depiction.
Listening to the discussions and the panels, searching for
the percussions of answers,
The bigger and deeper picture for what is beyond,
Trying to make sense of this fragile existence.
But there is only one who claimed to be the way, the truth,
the life,
The only one who can change your strife, your longing for
purpose.
Today is the day for your salvation, today is the day He
comes your way.
Questions have answers, but only He can fulfil.
He is the only one to say, "Peace, be still."
God's will, which was shrouded in mystery, is now proven
through His history.
Only He can create in your heart a new state.
Only He can make and change your fate.
Don't wait, don't delay. Joe, He waits for you. What do
you say?

'LITTLE MISS OWEN'

Little Miss Owen's,
Who has her own show on everything the media won't
cover.
When along came the haters,
Who were negated and debated,
And, of course, Candice scared them away.

'FANNY WILLIS'

Fanny Willis,
Die Hard like Cyphellis.
Treachery and contempt,
A definite attempt,
To persuade and portray.
Nothing to see here,
Trump needs to fear.
Election interference,
Is the point of difference,
Not funds that were splurged,
On their feelings, they were urged.
A past relationship before the contractor ship,
Surely it was professional, even with the calls and
messages.
Lots of testimony to attest of the facts,
Lots of testimony — they saw all their acts.
Now Congress involved — the long arm of the law.
Indictments, subpoenas — it is now getting raw.
Waiting for the truth, disqualified or reinstated —
We wait with bated breath
For history that's being created.

'DOUBLE THE CHRIS'

Double the Chris,
Double the bliss,
But all I hear seems hit and miss.
We all made our lists, they've checked them twice,
And all that I hear are dreams at a price.
I've watched the debates, they both seem like mates.
No one stands out, it seems down to fate.
Labor and National stand tall, don't fall,
But it seems so fractional, but it could be impactful.
Undecided and divisive, that's what I see,
Our nation in tatters, like our economy.
What is the answer, you ask so intrigued?
Well, I sit here also in ambiguity.
When truth meets honor, when there's no disparity,
You're halfway there to gaining clarity.

'BIDEN SHEEP'

Bah Bah Biden Sheep,
Are you really a fool?
Yes sir, yes sir,
I am under Biden's rule.
1 for Biden-nomics,
1 for student debt,
And 1 for his businesses that are paying all his debt.

'EGGS EGGS'

Eggs, eggs, we don't need to beg.
Eggs are so cheap I can eat them in my sleep.
They have come so far down that they're all over town.
Eggs, eggs, 60% drop since Biden was the top,
And all because of Trump's targets.
He's hitting them hard, there will be no regrets.
There's no mistaking now, I can have eggs and bacon!
Eggs, eggs, now the future is looking brighter,
Truly a reset to the current culture.
Things are looking different now, oh, how the Biden has
fallen!
Now the egg's on his face, Pam Bondi now calling.
The investigation now enthralling, as we watch, it's not
stalling.
Eggs, eggs could grow legs, but then begs the question:
"What comes first, the chicken or the egg?"

'LORD YOU ARE WONDER'

You place that coal to my lips,
To free me from my sin.
Your robe of light lets me come in.
You set a table for me, even when I'm not worthy.
My enemies are near, but your armor is sturdy.
Lord, you are wonder. Lord, you are grace.
I fall on my knees, waiting, it's never too late.
You seem so distant, even when you are near.
I try to listen and lose all my fear.
I need you now, Lord, but my mind is a spin.
I keep doubting myself because of my sin.
Lord, you are wonder. Lord, you are grace.
I fall on my knees, waiting, it's never too
late.
Your presence daily is what I need.
Everything else is pride and vanity.
I humble myself, my heart and my soul.
Return to me, Lord, and make me whole.
I am waiting and watching, reading your word,
Looking for answers, waiting to be heard.
Lord, you are wonder. Lord, you are grace.
I fall on my knees, waiting, it's never too late.
Lord, I am broken. Lord, set me free, Jesus, your peace and
your liberty.
Lord, never leave me.
Your Spirit I need.
Lord, in your presence,
Please let me be.

'DOCTOR JORDAN PEDERSEN'

Dr. Jordan Pedersen, a man with lots of wisdom,
Full of intellect and talks about people's idioms.
Now the Council of Canada have become an armada,
Trying to take away his speech, is it beyond their reach?
Still struggling with his faith, like all who walk that way,
Being called a Christian seems too hard to explain.
But God is spirit, true worship is this way,
Through His Son, the way, the truth, the life.
We confess and believe Him, then follow His light.
I have seen how you teach beyond the plain,
Seven rules that you have preached.
Many interviews, debates about pay gaps and gender
equality, Confused, it seems like a blender.
Return to sender with that rational.
This is your season for making an impact,
Young men are now finding themselves.
They have responded to your book, it has become a hook,
A rook in their personal armour.
Now, through your trials and situations,
You have risen with alleviation.
Understanding God and wisdom has infused your mind
To make you who you are today.
Your testimony is clear for those who have an ear.
Christ has cleared the way for you, so be of good cheer.
I say, "Kia Kaha," stand strong in your adversity,
When God has your back, you don't need a university.

'ANDREW BLOODY WILSON'

Andrew Wilson, like a pipe wrench Stilson.
Gripping the steel, wielding words that are real.
Uncompromising facts and stats, hard to match,
Debating the tools and schools them like fools.
Like a smoking gun tact, he extracts and exacts.
I can't help but laugh, but I truly feel sorry,
For these people who try to reach their own glory.
Keeping them in check is a job at its best,
But of course, he is better he rises to the test.

'ELON YOU DOGE'

Elon, you Doge, how dare you impose? why do you
suppose you have the right?
You weren't elected, even though directed by the president
elect to try and correct,
Stop what you're doing, you're crossing the line, personal
information your stealing, it's a crime.
We don't permit, it's not legit so, quit.
We sing, we'll stand, we'll impose our drama, we'll stand
in your face, and spit like a llama.
This will not end, this will not stop.
Nationalism is fascism, well commit all we've got.
So, Elon, you Doge. we're here to the end,
Democrats forever left of the bend.

'MY MESS IS YOUR MESSAGE'

The mess I'm in, keeps me stressing sin.
The way I kept, the road I took,
The path was wide, my soul it shook.
But you changed my heart, you made me whole.
You broke my shadows and paid the toll.

Jesus, daily renew my spirit.
Direct me Lord to always finish.
Let my life reflect your love and grace.
Lord, I live to love your ways

You delivered me from my insanity.
On the cross that day, you set me free.
Your peace you offer is beyond this world,
From the waves of the enemy that swirl and swirl.
Jesus, daily renew my spirit.
Direct me Lord to always finish.
Let my life reflect your love and grace.
Lord, I live to love your ways

'THE DEMS ARE COMING'

Raid the station,
They're part of our nation.
There's too much exploitation.
We need to push back.
Let's get Barack,
Let's get Chuck Schumer,
Let's get AOC, we should have done it sooner,
Don't push that line, don't cross our paths.
You'll be sorry walking on broken glass.
You can't keep winning, we simply won't let it.
We will protest to the end, so don't you forget it.
Theatrics and games that is our warfare.
We're now on the Podcasts, so everyone beware.
We won't hold back we'll keep on cunning, like a broken
record the Dems keep running.

'THE DEMS OF DRAMA'

Democrats are drama.
They spit like a llama,
In your face to cause a reaction and karma.
No truth to the emotion, where fiction is a faction,
With no actual traction.
Democrats are drama, but what they did has brought
harmer.
Making mountains out of molehills to break the people's
wills'
It instills nothing but frustration and nauseation of
exhaustion.
Democrats are drama, a new way, a new error.
Stop with actions, stop with the terror.

'WHY THE SABBATH'

You may ask, why the sabbath? what a task?
The one day that God blessed and sanctified, the one day
that I put aside.
The one day that God made holy,
The one day that we acknowledge,
That he is our God and we are his people.
After all, the sabbath is for our own temple.
We come and praise and worship our King,
The one who makes all our hearts sing,
The only one who fills my soul,
That sings my heart and makes me whole.
Never again to be alone, he rolled away the stone.
Forever the connection for me to God.
He stands in the gap and provides a way,
Through his suffering and through his shame.
I now stand blameless in his name.
What a joy and wander it is to know forever I am his.

'JACINDA ARDERN WHAT A CONCERN'

That your book on beliefs should give relief to the people
of our fine nation,
But instead, more questions about your intentions when
leading our country through Covid
A difficult time, where we were put on the line to showcase
your leadership skills, to make you shine.
In limbo we stood, we sat, we lay down,
We watched as the rest of the world went round.
As your implemented shutdowns, isolated cities, and even
little towns.
What went down then? You talked about unknowns,
experts were shown.
We listened to doctors, professionals in the field.
You said "Give up the liberty today you yield.
Stay at home keep your distance, stay safe.
Don't talk to your neighbours, or your friends, box yourself
like a crate.
Keep your hedge of protection, your selection of everyone
else"
What a Revelation, no, what forethought, what
understanding,
A visionary leader the times are demanding.
Aunty Jacinda, the nation named your persona.
We connected with this identity, it fuelled an aroma.
A sweet rising perfume,
That put us in a coma.
Then just like that, you ended, gone outta sight.
You said "It was time" and now it was right.

Left in the wake, families and communities
Nothing was safe, there were no immunities.
Everyone suffered and hindsight's a bugger.
The future looks dim, but hope and faith is our culture,
Like a sepulcher, it stands rock solid in our hands.
Our spirit of resilience, built on resistance.
We will never stop, we will never fall.
We will rise to our purpose, we will rise to our call.

'LORD ONLY YOU'

Free from my shame,
Free from my guilt.
Lord, only you can give me your grace.
Lord, only you I stand in awe.
Lord, only you can fulfil the law.
I lived according to myself.
Then all that disappeared,
When you erased all my doubt.
Lord, only you deserve all the glory.
Lord, only you can renew and rewrite my story.
Forgiveness, repentance, they live at your side.
You have renewed my heart and shown me my pride.
Lord, only you always impart.
I pray for your spirit to never depart.
Lord, only you can change my heart.
Never will you leave me, never will you part,
Lord, only you always change me.
I am living for today my past is history.
Lord, only you. You're coming again.
I look toward the day when there's no more pain.

'TWO GENDER TWO GENDER '

Two gender, two gender, to find a new sex.
Home again, home again, wreckety wrecked.
Two gender, two gender, something is wrong.
Home again, home again, singing this song.

'MEDIA BIAS'

CNN, MSNBC, ABC:
The true reporters of leftist liberty.
What a breakdown in communication,
When they can't even tell the nation.
When the truth of investigation becomes a secondary
alliteration.
Oh, truth where is thy sting.
Oh, liberal media you are dying.
The landscape is changing, anyone can be a reporter.
Journalism is subjective, which is why there's been
disorder.
The old days are gone, the narrative was strong,
But now they have been dissected,
The public is disconnected.
The illusion has been real,
Your minds, they tried to steal.
Your head was cooked and sifted,
Now the paradigm has shifted.
The news is being gifted,
By the average man on the ground,
It is quite a deafening sound.
To the channels losing viewers.
The people have spoken, there's no more fancy lures.

'TRUMPETS FROM ELON'

Elon's musk is trumpeting Trump's task,
But how, you may ask?
The once symphonic relationship is now a bubonic
battleship.
But these things happen when man's pride is at stake,
Things are said to the decisions you make.
Does that mean it's over for the team that shook the
swamp?
The team that took a chomp of avenues for the revenues,
That cut the needless spending,
Which carried on amending, and now there's no more
bending?
But with the nation at stake, these men will not fake
How important it is to stay on the biz.
So continue to fight, to do what is right,
And keep the nation's future always in sight.

'MORNING STAR HAS BROKEN'

I can offer you money,
I can offer you pride.
I can make you very powerful if you just take my side.
If you fall down and worship, everything you dreamed can
soon be yours,
But you have to give me your heart and soul so I can be
your core.
I will give you all those fancy things; if you fall on your
knees, I will even give you wings,
To make you fly so high.
Forget about those other things that are burning your desire.
Your spirit may diminish, but I'll give you new attire.
The old man can stay; he is welcome in my way.
No need to change your efforts, live only for today.
Do what you want, it's good.
Don't worry about desire for the one you should.
All that glistens is gold, those things I can withhold.
No need to search deeper, no need to look within.
Don't worry about tomorrow, don't worry about your sin.
My path is very wide, you can always travel on it.
I'll make you forget who you are and think there's nothing
beyond it.
Your cares and your worries, I can give you something
better.
The things of this world will become your chains and
fetters.
You'll live with the fear of death, because I never created
your rest.
But the bells, toys, and whistles, they are the best.

So don't worry about tomorrow, live for my today.
I'm the one who controls this world; I'm the one, so do
what I say.

'GOD IS GOOD'

God is good all the time.
Time is good when you're in God's light.
It's never dark, because He shines bright.
The goodness of God is always in sight.
He walks before us in the shadows of night,
Never to leave us, He makes us right.
His timing is perfect, even when we are not worth it.
The goodness of God continues to search us,
To beckon us forward in moments of peace.
He'll never leave us, puts our hearts at ease.
He continues to work on our minds and heart.
His Spirit is guiding us through the dark.
The goodness of God will never fail.
His timing is perfect, He'll put the wind back in your sail.
In every detail, in every minute, the Great I Am is always
in it.
There's not a time when God is never not.
Check your life, every moment, every minute.
He's never left you, so keep your chin up.
Run the race, because He'll be on time.
He'll return and say, "Welcome, faithful, you are mine."

'ETERNITY IN OUR HEARTS'

Eternity in our heart,
Right from the start.
He created us with this as part of our being,
This was connected right from the beginning.
Our longing to be, which is part of our unity.
He formed us and knew us before we were born;
Our ins and outs, to's and fro's, up's and downs.
But forever is found in our being and thoughts,
An immortal elixir, for the world is a fixer.
But the one who holds time uses this as a sign,
That the longing to be, for you and me,
Is part of our make-up, our DNA, the key.
So no more wondering or meandering—he gives you the
reason
To seek him and know him beyond every season.
One day he'll declare—I pray we'll be there,
That moments upon moments were built for us to share.
His will, not ours; his purpose as well:
"Well done, faithful servant, now enjoy your crown."

'BUD LIGHT OH WHAT A FRIGHT'

Bud Light, Bud Light,
Oh what a fright.
Stocks went down and now are out of sight.
A certain narrative, a certain agenda,
Taking a stance on identity and transgender.
You tried to redeem your original status,
Too late for the changes, now everything's in tatters.
Did everyone else learn from your position?
Did everyone learn that it's not a competition?
You have been sunken by this treason, this reason, your
choice
To deliver your voice on such a controversial point.
It has clearly showed that your views are out of joint.
The rest of the populace aren't a part of this directive.
Don't push it, don't prop it,
This unpopular narrative.
Let people confirm in what they stand firm.
Go back to your roots, boots on the ground.
The traditional route is a judgement that's sound.

'SPIRIT ARE YOU IN IT'

Are you flesh or are you spirit?
Do you know whether if you're in it?
What controls you is what matters,
The way you see people, the things that happen.
Love is the strongest bond,
We are given, it's in our hands.
Peace and freedom can be ours
If on the solid rock we stand.
Days, months, and even years,
The flesh steals from us; it never hears.
It never listens and draws us in,
It always conquers us with sin.
The guilt and shame seem like a game,
But they hold us down like a weighted train.
A perilous situation, a stagnant state beyond repair,
You have to repent before it's too late, don't leave it in the
air.
Time is of the essence. Don't tarry, don't wait; He'll show.
You need to dwell in His presence to find your best flow.
For we are flesh covered in spirit; we were from the
beginning.
The separation from Him stops our true living.
We are shadows that dance around the ever-shining light,
We live in constant darkness until He changes our plight.
Only the Word can brighten the way, He longs to be part of
your every day.
He understands your needs and fears;
He has seen all your heartache and tears.

He knocks and waits for your answer,
Waiting to abide, no second chances.
Today is salvation, not tomorrow or a later date.
He's ready to take your burdens; He's ready to take your
weight.
Spirit, you need to be in it.
In the end there's only One.
He's coming soon, I promise,
Don't remain a prodigal son.

'HEY DIDDLE DIDDLE'

Hey diddle diddle,
The White House was a riddle.
The media went to the moon.
The other countries laughed to see such fun,
Then China ran away with the spoon.

'ICE ICE BABY'

Ice, ice, baby, Gavin Newsom is crazy.
Bass is acting cagey,
L.A. is looking hazy.
Once again, it's common sense that trumps with a
rearguard offense.
Having to militarize the army,
Against the crime that is so balmy.
You say you want to stay here,
In the city of L.A.,
But you parade every day another flag, then you say: "Not
USA — not us, not today."
The Red, White & Blue is due a good review,
It's a symbol for patriots to hold fast and true.
The one they should always declare and share,
The one that invokes so much emotion and fear.
This is the one that should have your devotion,
But no, you protest with the silliest of notions.
"Peacefully and lawfully," you say to no end,
But your actions and your voices never show that trend.
The decision has been made, the troops won't delay.
It's a mess in L.A., but we know it's okay.
The administration will end the chaos that's at hand,
Peace will be enacted.
Finally, common sense will stand.

'VIVEK IS ON FLEEK'

Vivek Ramashwamy,
Direct like an army.
Called the last election,
Fake by detection.
A story not given, a story not shared,
Fact-checked by people who didn't even care.
Vivek is on fleek,
With his points that critique,
Ready to talk, ready to discuss,
Anywhere, anyone, he knows it's a must.
Political conversation that's never going to rust.
He is data-driven, that's what's on the table.
He is happy to concede if your facts you are able.
He could see that a breath of fresh air is needed.
He injected himself; his advice should be heeded.

'GREG GUTFELD IS NOT FROM LEFTFIELD'

Greg Gutfeld, far from left field, as you see on his show,
With entertaining quips and lashes of brutality.
His centrality of issues is never neutrality,
A calm dismantling of what the left are chanting.
This slanting narrative, this shouting and ranting,
Can seem enchanting, but Greg has them recanting
Their thoughts on The View,
Always a take on their verbal spew.
With a joke and a laugh, he curtails the cast,
What a blast from the vast array of information.
I cannot watch all, I must confess,
Because of my Christian call, it's not always best.
But when I do, I smile and laugh along too,
Greg Gutfeld, one of the choices of voices I cue.

'THANK YOU FOR BEING A FRIEND'

Trump and Epstein like a Chinese chow mein,
What a mixture, a debacle; does this make him lose his
sparkle?
From the friendship, the connection,
Which seems now under protection.
The closets, the shadows, which we all try to hide,
But the digital footprint always steps inside.
We are all vulnerable to this very collection,
Dissection of our lives which we all try to hide.
The truth always rises, ugly or not.
It can set you on a collision with division and rot.
We know what Epstein stood for, the evil he subjected,
And now he is gone, things are being dissected.
In this life, what remembers you are not the material
reflections,
But the relationships with people, with family, those
connections.
Our digital footprint is so easy to find,
What we have done, what we do, those things we can't
hide.
We cannot defend it, but accept we were wrong.
Own up and own it, these stay forever. That's long.
You can't unsend what has been done.
The messages between them linked an unwritten song.
The impact this has affects Trump's shine.
I must admit, even for me, this is a sign.
But no one is perfect, we all make mistakes.
It's the defense of these wrongs, to deny all the takes.

Admission is not submission, accountability is important.
Either it's true or it's a lie,
After all, someone died.
What will be the conclusion? Is this another Russia collusion?
The pictures, the videos, the testimony are ridiculous.
The outcome cannot be distorted or contorted, these holds are reported.
We watch, we wait, we discuss, we debate.
At the end of the day, either you accept it or not,
This connection, their friendship, like a sign, it's the wrong way.
We sit with bated breath. In the end, truth will have its say.

'AUTO PEN, WHAT DO YOU KNOW'

Auto pen, Auto pen, what do you know?
Why are you so quiet? You're on the Biden show.
You who once held esteem and prominence,
A magical mystique who has confounded the networks.
Now investigated for what you have done,
There'll be no hiding place in the shadows, in the sun.
The truth will come out in a roundabout way,
Everyone will see in the light of day,
The way you disguised, the way you misrepresented,
The way you fooled Biden, who was the president.
You signed so many pardons, maybe even documents;
Justice will come swiftly for those planted innocents.
The fate of the nation, for justice and transparency,
Now sits in the wake of lost democracy.
Well, Auto pen, the jury is out,
You are found guilty without a shadow of a doubt.

'RIVER OF LIFE'

Oh river of life that flows from Christ,
The thirst where my soul can remain in the light.
When I drink of this water, my heart is at rest,
My soul is at peace, I am at my best.
The one true source for living, of course,
Flows from the man with nails in his hand.
He gently woo's with His love, He calls with His grace,
The love in His eyes, His character you trace.
Oh, living wate, nothing can replace.
There is nothing to compare,
There is nothing to fear.
Living waters of Jesus that flow from the throne,
The water comes down when we are His own.
Living waters of life, come flow into me.
Spirit of Christ, I need sanctity.

'WHEN WILL IT END'

When will it end?
When will time resend?
For generations and millennia, the world has always stood,
For men that were evil, for men that were good.
Only one constant factor, only one thing always heard,
One thing always remembered, that's God's constant
Word.
He spoke through the prophets, through kings in the past,
But now, through His Son, His Spirit has been cast,
To convict the world in truth and show His righteousness,
To change our hearts to light, to bring us out of the
darkness.
He will never leave you; He provides a way through the
blood that was shed.
Jesus calls you today.
Every day you don't accept, every day you don't open,
The door remains closed because you think that you are
coping.
It's a day you have lost in guilt and shame,
The Devil lays upon you because it's part of his game.
Look beyond the physical, look beyond this world.
God's Spirit is calling, His Son is the pearl.
Don't think it won't happen; faith is a step.
We all have certain questions, but only He knows what's
next.
So don't tarry, don't wait, your race is limited at best.
When you live without Jesus, your burdens weigh you
down in a nest.
Your conscience of sins pins you from within.

He is coming back soon, so make sure you're ready.
Every knee will bow, every tongue confess
That Jesus died so you could be blessed.

'HICKORY DICKORY DOCK'

Hickory Dickory Dock,
Covid was a shock.
The clock has won,
It took all our fun.
Hickory Dickory Dock.

'THE FIVE IS ALIVE'

The Five is alive like a beehive of activity.
There is not much sensitivity, but creativity to match.
The dynamics with Jessie, Greg, and Dana,
The things they talk about are not insane.
With Harold and Jessica, sometimes Emily,
Thoughtfully and tactfully, they make points exactly.
But the one that is most missed, who brings the legal fist:
Judge Janine Pirro, who I would say is my hero.
Who cuts through the jargon to show the left's far gone.
The Five is still alive and will thrive,
But I miss the dynamics, the haptics that I wore like a
ChapStick.
But the Judge is needed and is seated in the District of
Columbia,
Now the attorney on a journey for the Trump
administration.
Nevertheless, for the press I confess,
The stories provide and collide with pride; they strive to
decide the truth that's inside.
So, to The Five, the beehive of free thinking and
discussion,
Carry on sounding the common-sense percussion.

'LEFTIES HAVE LOST IT'

Rita Panahi
Lefties losing their pan-ities,
Becoming unhinged with TDS syringed.
The Karens and the Kens—oh when will it end?
Having to apologize for dissatisfied factions,
The people now acting as segmented rations.
So much material for your segment and reel,
I suspect the content will never lose its appeal.
As long as there's feeling alive in this world,
There'll always be confusion—boy or girl?
A whole month of antics from the smallest percent,
So beautiful, they say, for our kids to gain "heritage" intent.
What a wonderful collage of color and sexuality,
Our kids should be watching to form their identity.
No matter the age, for they all understand,
Confusion is normal since men aren't men,
Women are men, and girls are boys.
Each for their own, don't gender the toys.
"Love is love," we hear this a lot,
But only when biology doesn't define the zygote.
So let's all play nicely, genes and biology,
Lefties losing it shows you don't need chronology.

'STAY IN THE FIGHT'

Stay in the fight,
Not the left or the right,
Run that race,
Be guided by the light.
Stay in the fight.
Don't give up, don't lose hope,
The one who is working in you
Will keep you afloat.
Fight on, fight always, says He, the Ancient of Days.
Fight on, fight peacefully.
Stay in the fight.
Being good or being bad,
Don't turn around.
He knows and He cares.
Let His Spirit guide you,
Let His love take you there.
Follow His leading, His grace will appear.
Lord, I anguish from hurt, all of my pain.
I seek You daily, again and again.
Clear my mind, change my heart,
Refresh me daily, set me apart.
Let me fight the good fight,
Let me run the right race.
Let me see You, Jesus,
Cover me by Your grace.
"Stay in the fight," You whisper to me,
"Stop fighting My Word, let it set you free."
Lord, Your Word is a double-edged sword.
It pierces the heart of those that have heard.

Stay in the fight, right till the end,
I am waiting to see You come back again.
Glory, oh glory, to the One who is right.
Lord, You are perfect, Your Son is the light.
Refresh me daily to stay in the fight.
I am waiting and watching — Lord, guide my sight.

'BILL MAHER THE SAYER'

Bill Maher is a sayer of political sorts.
While he sports his opinions, he directs his reactions.
He's left of the middle, but not left in insanity.
He's been around long enough to know where the Dems are languishing.
Now he's seen the capitulation, they're breaking at the seams.
Comedy and politics he forks, while the Dems are still in dreams.
With a relaxed combination, he creates a solid connection,
Creating direction on any section, maybe he's defecting.
He loves America with no end in sight, with all its constant layers, even though it's not right.
Bill Maher, the sayer that doesn't hold back, he knows what he knows and never holds back.

'THE TESTIMONY OF JESUS'

The spirit of prophecy has always dictated history,
Because it was a mystery before Jesus was revealed.
The way he lived, loved, and healed, upon him, Holy Spirit
sealed.
He will shield us from the evil one,
But we still come undone, that's why we remain in the Son.
Prophecies that he has fulfilled,
Things written long ago by people who did God's will,
Of man's comings to and fro,
To show that he is real, what he did is now an appeal.
Sin was forever defeated, and Jesus is now seated
By his Father at the right hand, and now we are able to
stand,
In his presence and in his sight, because Jesus makes us
right.
His testimony lives out in our very lives,
Because we accept him in our hearts, the Spirit sanctifies.
He wants to make us whole,
To keep us free from Sheol,
To set us apart and holy for that specific goal.
We live in contrast to this world, in every moment and
every season.
We love differently, consistently, persistently, that's our
song.
Jesus testifies for us in the sanctuary because we're wrong,
Until the Father says, "Enough sin has filled its cup."
An end to sin, it is needed.
The door is no more open; your testimony has sealed it.

He who is righteous is righteous still.
The works of the hardened heart have their will.
"I am coming, my reward is with me,
For your works of love I've seen.
Now is the day of your salvation,
Don't tarry, don't slumber, don't wait.
Don't wait for tomorrow, for tomorrow might be too late."

'INCY WINCY HILLARY'

Incy Wincy Hillary climbed the political spout.
Down came Russia gate and washed poor Hillary out.
Out came the emails and showed up all the lies.
Incy Wincy Hillary climbed up the spout again.

'GAS LIGHTING IS FRIGHTENING'

Gas lighting, what a frightening display, with an array of
words often heard.
This term is not endearing, because it's not worth sharing.
If you are in this position, it causes frustration, a mutation
of feelings that are propagated and stated.
This feeling of uncertainty by placing you in absurdity,
To question yourself, your understanding, and identity.
Apparently I do this, my kids sometimes say; I'm unsure of
the context, they have to explain.
Wherever you sit, when you look at it literally,
Gas lighting can capitulate an individual with words.
It's certainly not articulate or circumspect; it seems more
divisive and derives from igniting.
It causes inciting and never stops implying.

'WHAT A TRAP THIS WORLD IS'

What a trap this world is, with the glistening and gold.
The bells and the whistles are temporary, you know.
What will you leave? What is your legacy?
The people you leave, the relationship activity.
Or do you think that the material things will sing your
praise, will remember your giving, your way of living?
Chains and fetters, this world never gets better.
Everything is vanity; it all ends in tatters.
No matter your wealth, your gains, and your status,
What remains are the people, the links, the chatter.
Time in their presence, you soaked up their essence.
They shared with you history, mysteries unfold.
Were you listening? Were you present? Were you
hastening the day?
Did you understand what this world has no offer but
A burden, a weight, no time to stay?
Did you make today all that it should be
By loving the people around you, beside you, what fate.
No debate on the issue, people are a true love source.
They take you to the ends of your tethers, of course.
But love is truly defined by the people who love you, the
ones you left behind.

'LORD I NEED YOU TODAY'

Today, oh Lord, is not my day.
I am feeling sad and not feeling okay.
If you please, could you remind me of your love and grace,
And then come and see me, maybe face to face?
I am needing the joy that your spirit only gives.
I am out here struggling, trying just to live.
"Share my faith," you say, but I am in disarray.
My heart is in decay, then you tell me just to pray.
I am with you always, even to the end.
The Helper will be with you when you're going off the
bend.
My word is always with you, through the Helper who's
been left.
The enemy is always prowling, roaring to take you down.
Just remember who's victorious, and who will give you
your crown.

'WE ARE ALL THE SAME'

Can a man be a woman, and can a woman be a man?
Can a father be a mother, and a mother be a father?
Is this the next step in the evolutionary track?
Do we swap our genders when there's no looking back, cop
the flack, then start to attack?
Gender fluidity is not confusion; words migrate, and I have
my conclusion.
This is my truth and my way, not tomorrow, but today.
Affirmation, I do not need confirmation that you agree.
You cannot change my mind; I have my declaration.
This is not a sensation or an emotional discussion,
My intuition is not a recreational drug,
Or a bug that disappears. We have been here for years. In
cultures and tribes, we have always altered the vibes.
Indigenous cultures have always been fluid between the
roles, not from magic, not from druids.
The future is clear; history is now in the rear.
We are nearer than ever to human repair.

'MEGAN GUN KELLY'

The Megan Gun Kelly Show will blow the leftist insanity.
Please stop the flow of bereft, let's turn and watch Hannity.
Putting facts and stats, such a clear, tactful track,
Never amiss calling it out,
Even Tapper got a schlack.
Megan Gun Kelly, like a six-gun on the hip,
Fast to the draw, many a quip has caused a trip.
A quick-draw McCaw that strikes to the core,
A targeted direction for the leftist insane selection.
Reloading the ammo, always quick and never slow,
Megan Gun Kelly, you draw with ease.
Your weapon of choice takes them to their knees.
There are no typos, it's concise and effective,
Marshalling the facts, it's not predictive.
The show must go on, and you are never short.
There are stories and talking points that you never contort.
You sort through the rubbish to reveal the true source.
You never back down like some around town.
So, stay the course for the nation,
Remain always in the fight,
True to yourself, and to do what is right.
Machine Gun Kelly, you never fail
To exact the truths of the stories with the facts to match.

'I STAND WITH ISRAEL'

I stand with Israel, He never forgot Ishmael.
I pray for blessings on his people, the apple of his eye.
I stand with Israel; our God will never lie.
Throughout the world's history, what remained was a
mystery.
What was the point of Gods' will, which seemed kept until,
The savior was revealed from previously being concealed?
God was presented; the word became flesh.
His way of loving people is always the best.
Not feelio, but agape is what we need to mesh.
His mercy and forgiveness, through his spirit, we are
blessed.
I stand with Israel regardless of what others say.
His bond with his people through his remnant has always
stayed.
His everlasting covenant to the remnant that remained,
Never will he leave.
Jesus showed the people the way.
He gave them every opportunity to be called by his name.
He healed the blind, the deaf, and also the lame,
The lost, the last, and the least, the reason why he came.
I stand with Israel.
My heart is for his people, my spirit he has reset, but my
flesh is very feeble.
I stand with Israel forever and a day.
He is coming very soon, so always watch and pray.

'STORMY SEAS & JACK DANIEL'S'

Stormy Daniels,
Like Cocka Spaniels,
Bigger than a bite,
With things that go bump in the night.
An illicit exploitation,
Of a supposed situation,
Hush money revelation
Of the publicized relations.
Complications in a conviction because of the depiction,
On a trial that points to another distraction.
Nobody is falling for the fatal attraction.
Time and delay is the only tool on display.
The circus of information is clearly a play.
Will justice, will patriotism, Trump on the day?
We watch and we wait and only anticipate.

'A TIME FOR YOU AND ME'

When the week is over and I'm feeling overrun,
I'm glad that you've given a blessing for everyone.
The promise has never changed,
A time of Godly rest.
Lord, it's time to worship and feed our spiritual nest.
Miracles and wonders is what you'll will see
When the God of creation meets with you and me.
We are so thankful for this time, a time of Godly rest.
Let's all come together and worship the one who's best.
There is none like you, oh Lord, you're the Great I Am.
You were there at the beginning, you'll be there at the end.
You never tire or weary, but you knew that we would.
You are always working wonders and doing all the good.
Your promises are forever, your Word is always true.
The Sabbath, made in Heaven, is one for me and you.
We need your Godly rest, it's been there from the start.
When we enter your Godly rest, you refresh our weary
hearts.
Join us as we say, come worship on this day,
A day of Godly rest, a day that God has made.
You never tire or weary, but you knew that we would.
You are always working wonders and doing all the good.
Your promises are forever, your Word is always true.
The Sabbath, made in Heaven, is one for me and you.

'JASMINE CROCKETT WHAT A ROCKET'

Jasmine Crockett, what a rocket, another crazy notion.
So much pent up of your inside emotion.
The facts don't make sense to the narrative she sends.
Left-leaning Dems, when will it end?
Voicing the disparities from decades of old,
Let's move forward, don't put things on hold.
This apparently is the Dems' new mold.
Breaking the new blue could be proving a boo boo.

'SPORTS AND POLITICS WHAT A MIX'

Sports and politics, should they mix?
Do they fix or address any situation that plagues any
nation?
Do they highlight the plight of the cultures and struggles,
For the people on the ground, for the people who are
sluggers,
Battling to be the best, to overcome and beat the rest?
I detest the cauldron of emotions
That is depicted by this commotion.
Keep it separate, I say, for the respect of all who train and
compete.
Don't change the mindset of people who meet,
To support and be entertained.
What is gained by voicing your position,
When your sport, your training is only for competition?
Why should others be subjected by the position you
selected?
The history of sports was not to be distorted,
Or contorted by individuals who thought that their platform
should be a place to inform,
About what they believe, or the understanding they've
received.
It's a very sad day, which adds to the decay, for the reason
why sport was invented,
Camaraderie and competition, respect and elation,
Losers and celebration.
This is a journey to build an individual,
A group of people connecting,

Through the sport that's been selected,
Affected by the spirit of intrinsic value given to me and
you,
Through the equality of rules, which politics doesn't have.
So, save sports.
Leave it alone.
Let it entertain.
Let it be a beacon, a home of spectatorship,
Of oohs and aahs,
Not of gotcha moments.
Let the moments replay as legacies of lives,
From people who strived to compete and thrive.

'THE MIDDLE EAST WHAT A BEAST'

The Middle East, what a beast, a tirade of foreign mish
mash.
A disaster of biblical proportion.
It's propaganda that's the distortion.
Israel is under attack from the left, the right, to keep them
off track. There's no letup, like a monkey on their back.
Arrows keep coming, the information is cunning.
The lies, the distortions, the contortions of truth.
This is not physical, it's a spiritual tool.
From the river to the sea is chanted to set them free.
But what about the Jews, where's their right indeed?
Their history is worth researching, your mind will be set
free.
But Israel is Gods' covenant, he will never leave them, see.
Bless those who bless them, but a curse to those who don't.
God will never leave them, for the remnant always at home.

'WHY OH WHY LORD'

Lord, why the suffering? Why the loss?
Why is life death, and why the cross?
Why does my life matter?
Why do I need to count the cost?
If nothing matters, why do I feel like this?
My heart misses something , nothing physical, it's in my
spirit,
Longing for peace, longing for rest, longing to know what's
beyond the test.
Why are you silent, oh Lord? Why do you not answer?
I have been living my life, waiting for those chances
To break free from this world when all that glistens isn't
gold.
But still nothing, oh Lord, why make me wait? No answers,
even when I pray.
How long, oh Lord, will I feel this way? Please, I pray, feel
my anguish, feel my pain.
I love you. You say through your Word, that's the place
you reassure me you'll never leave, that's the place for
understanding, for wisdom, for fear,
Where you say you are always near, right beside me.
You'll carry me if I choose to believe, that's the way to
receive.
So many examples, so many testimonies, so many people
who were changed throughout history.
I bring my heart to your feet, I lay my burdens like a sleet.
I am open and bare, Lord, can you clear the road, true and
still, so I can surrender my will
To fulfill why you made me?

For your purpose I trade me, my flesh and my ways,
To live out my days in your presence, your essence. Lord, I
need
Lord, daily to be free. I will set my mind on you through
prayers on bended knee.
I will seek through the storms; I will search when I am in
need.
Lord, clean my sin. Holy Spirit, set me free.

'BAA BAA BARACK SHEEP'

Baa baa Barack sheep, have you any proof?
No sir, no sir, but I can break the rules.
One for the Democrats, 1 for the mules,
And 1 for the Diddy parties, swimming in the pools.

'WHAT IS BEING MAORI'

What is being Maori, I hear you say?
Is it Whakapapa, Tangata Whenua, all day, all the way?
Is it a moko or haka, the way you row your waka?
Do you look deeper within to see people, not of colour,
brown or olive skin?
Colonized and assimilated, it's part of our history.
We were highest on the caste system, that's not a mystery.
For family and community is part of our identity.
Gardening, gathering, and hunting, of course, were part of
our make-up to supply our food source.
But that seems long ago, it seems we stopped adapting.
It seems like things are against us, but we are not spiritual
captives.
We were created to be effective connectors, directed from
above.
We are receptors of a Wairua that was brought to us
through love.
Ask our prophets of old, who grew in the Word and were
bold.
God showed them a different way to be a part of His fray
till their end,
At the detriment of the people, sometimes to no end.
We are better from their actions colonized, but Christ-
connected.
This is reflected, it's not retrospective,
Effective on a spiritual plain. The latter rain is not physical,
it's an anointing for an appointed time,
The name of Jesus on everyone's heart and mind,
To leave the old man behind, to change what's inside,

To give you a new choice, a new will, an inspired voice
that calms you still.
TYJ, above the world You always reign. We know, You
are coming again, no more sorrow, no more pain.
Come, Jesus, come. Are you ready? This I pray.

'AUNTY JACINDA'

Jacinda Ardern, who was very stern,
Changed policy and laws.
Through lockdowns, she seemed worried and concerned.
We became scared even talking face to face, what a
disgrace.
You were so scared, you even brought some mace.
Vaccinated and scarred, we talked from afar.
Masked and mandated, everything seemed dark.
So now, in hindsight, we can see oh so well,
Science, was it followed? Only time will tell.

'LETITIA JAMES REGIN IT IN'

Letitia James, oh what a name.
She is now in shame for her part in the game.
Discredit Trump, make him a chump, "This illegitimate
president, I'll make him a dump!"
But now her error,
Is causing her terror.
She ran on, enthused,
TDS was infused.
She now stands accused and is going to lose.
Clinical mistake is now her rouse.

'CAPTAIN CHARLIE KIRK'

Captain Charlie Kirk of the Starship Faith and Clarity,
When debating others, which causes them disparity.
In the campuses, where critical thinking is a secondary inkling,
It seems quite radical and very superficial that the ideologies held are credible
When compared with the facts and all the stats. When it's broken down simply, that is that.
Yes, good points are risen, but when compared with history, can they be given?
Can they be accepted as valid and poignant, or are they divisive, emotive, and negative?
Feelings aren't facts, they are a hidden agenda that stands and propagates the left-wing bender.
Let's go back to chaos and drama, let's break the doors, let's spit like llamas.
"But Charlie, you have no degree, you aren't as smart as me."
No, I have something better, a lived world experience and books by the letter.
You stand in the way of mediocre thinking, of a far-left opinion that leaves people blinking.
I salute you, sir, and your determined ethics, to fight for the cause and battle the leftists.

'THOMAS SOWELL ECONOMIST EDUCATOR'

Thomas Sowell, who doesn't bode well for the left-wing
ideas,
An economist of economy proportion who counteracts all
the left's distortion.
So much wisdom, with much understanding,
The mind of a generation, with intellect to match.
Being blessed by his words of truth that connect,
His take on people's motives and hidden agendas,
Help me understand why the Dems can't render.
Ability beyond belief, common sense is their grief.
They are falling so far behind, with no let-up in sight,
And all they come up with is, "We are going to fight."
So thank you, Thomas, what a blessing you are,
Shining like a star. By far, you have set the bar.

'MEDIA HAD A LITTLE PLAN'

Media had a little plan, a little, a little plan, Media had a
little plan
To fleece us white as snow.
Everywhere the media would go,
Media would go, media would go,
Everywhere the media would go, the lies would somehow
follow.
They followed them for tools one day, tools one day, tools
one day.
They followed them for tools one day, then broke the
golden rule.
And now they're all in disarray, disarray, disarray, now
they're all in disarray, the media and their decay.

'ROCK STEADY'

Be ready, rock steady.
Don't turn, don't run.
The one who shakes the mountains,
God's only begotten Son.
He is knocking on your door,
He is breaking all your chains,
He is coming back victorious to conquer all the pain.
Don't wait for tomorrow,
Because tomorrow never comes.
Today, His grace, His calling. Today is the race you run.
Don't hold on to your past,
Don't be chained to your sin.
Open the door to your heart
And let the Spirit in.
It's time for a change, the world never fulfils.
Don't let it swallow you whole, don't take that bitter pill.
He is knocking, can't you hear?
His peace will calm your fear.
He is waiting to set you free,
Seek Him on bended knee.
Your life has gone so fast,
There is only one that clears your past.
The Three that are a witness, the Tri-unal God in One.
He's the one to redeem through His only begotten Son.

'SWAMP THING'

Another indictment,
Another incitement,
That's four on the go for the mighty Trump show.
Another block, another brick in the wall,
When all they are doing is causing their downfall.
Love him or hate him, he makes people believe,
That when it comes to America, everyone can achieve.
Clearing the swamp, a promise that he made,
Draining the swamp of the masquerade.
When's the next indictment? Who will be next?
It's political partisanship, let's put it in context.

'SANCTIFY ME LORD'

Sanctify my heart.
Make me sacred and set apart.
Mercy and grace cover me,
Your blood has set me free.
My eyes are blind and my ears are deaf.
I've been trying to find you, but I have nothing left.
I can't see through the shadows,
The darkness is looming.
Satan is prowling, he's growling and grooming.
The harder I try, the further I go,
Into the unknown, away from your truth.
Your Spirit, oh Lord, to help me finish.
Your Spirit, oh Lord, to keep me in it.
Run the race you set for me.
Stop being absent, so I fall on my knees.
Your presence daily is what I need,
Your presence daily to water the seed.
Caught in a lie,
That I thought was a sign,
Now I'm going backwards down that slippery slide.
The work of a lifetime,
You created in me.
You gave me purpose,
In my heart, eternity.
Never take your presence or essence from my life,
Because it's you, Jesus, you're the reason why.

'PARTISAN PARTISAN'

Partisan politics,
It turns people into Molotovs.
No getting along, no listening to the facts.
Here comes the information, let's get emotional, stat!
Why can't we get along, have a conversation, sing the same song?
Disagree but compromise, look at what we are saying, then compare and start praying.
Truth is undeniable, a foundation built on faith.
There is only one who showed the ultimate way,
A claim that He made, a road He made.
Forsaking His glory, He forgave our mistakes.
A clash of ideologies, a thrust of circumstances,
He was the one who stopped all the ordinances.
Let's try that lens that I see.
Bi-partisan, I reckon, will help you and me.

'THREE DAYS OF SEPERATION'

Three days of separation,
Three days of divination,
The act of salvation that came from the Lord on high.
The enactment of a plan that included Revelation,
The suffering and the shame, he healed the blind and lame.
He showed how to love the people, the reason why he
came.
He showed us humility and care so we can do the same.
Some say, "What a prophet, what a teacher!"
But he was always more than that, I am trying to beseech
ya.
If these three days had never been fulfilled,
If Jesus had done his own personal will,
My Christian life would never matter;
My hope and faith are firmly shattered.
But historians can't disprove three days that show the truth,
My life is built on nothing less,
But Jesus Christ and his righteousness.

'SENATOR SAS HAWLEY'

Senator Josh Hawley,
So concise, so surely,
Producing the facts and the stats to match.
Dismantling the lies to expose their narratives.
Through their positions, they cause these disparities.
The responses are priceless, the filibusters are endless,
But you never whine from your elected duty.
The truth you persist, a reason not to desist.
You resist the mist, the haze of delusion,
To always come to a precise conclusion.
Amidst the confusion, you rise as a solution,
The voice of reason, of logic and sense.
There's no let-up, so stay focused, stay on offense.
Common sense as a rule, which you use as a tool.
So keep it directed, use it as fuel.
Emotions aren't facts, and neither are feelings,
So keep raising the direction, lift the bar to the ceiling.

'DAVID SEAMORE BUTTS'

David Seamore butts, refutes and rebuts,
That his policies couldn't be unfair.
"No, they are not one-sided, because the country is divided,
On all his party's important issues," he says.
Address the inequality for most New Zealanders,
Who have no ability to discern the reality of what is
happening to them.
Instead, change history to effect any future mystery,
So we can move forward as a society, a united entity.
Do you really want our opinion, even though you've
formed your own?
Now you are known as that guy!
Who has made a lot of people sigh, maybe even cry.
Do you understand our plight?
Our founding document, Te Tiriti o Waitangi,
Which makes us inoculant, that gives us equality
From our colonised system.
Assimilation was its destination.
What is equal and what is fair?
With history so divided, it's our future that's in despair.
Making it easy to make more revenue
Just means, for us, a longer benefit queue.
Making our land available to mine,
Everything for money, fast-tracked for time.
Well, I'm not saying I have the answer,
Railroading your process will cause an angry cancer.
More time for public discourse, please.
Don't put us in a position where we are begging on our
knees.

Let's come together for the fate of the nation.
Money is not the answer, it's better ideas for production.
Let's embrace to enhance it.
You said you just wanted discussion,
But your motives were already in motion.
What we say will not matter, your agenda is clearly combative.

'RUSSIA RUSSIA'

Russia, Russia, what a crusher
An undermining attachment that came with an
impeachment.
What kind of treatment? A divisive concealment,
Then a media revealment,
A blitz of publicity to impose negativity,
To cause the direction of a most definite deflection.
So after all the hype and the propaganda, the truth is
coming out, Tulsi Gabbard demands it.
So who was in charge, and why the investigation?
Russia, of course, this is no inflation.
They rigged the election for the fate of the nation.
Trump, of course, was Putin's packhorse,
His golden ticket to put him in the thicket, to stick it to
America.
That couldn't be clearer… or that's what was portrayed.
The game they played with our emotions,
They strung us along with conceivable notions.
And as always, the truth has come out.
We're not in the darkness, there's no shadow of a doubt.

'I AM THAT I AM'

The foolish things of this world
Which still baffle the wisest of souls.
The Lord knows,
He sees where you're at, your purpose, your call.
You cast your pearls before the swine,
To work and contrive for material all.
You hold the stars in your hand,
And hang the planets on nothing.
You confound the wise with the smallest of things,
That try all their understanding.
In a world where we constantly seek,
To understand why things look so bleak,
Is a constant reminder of the One who remains,
And is always the same.
It is He who only and ever sustains.
To give you free will, and then love you still,
Through all of your pain, suffering, and shame.
You're the reason He came.
He still calls you by name.
His love for you, through His Son, He sees,
Only the best version, where you remain free.
Free from guilt, free from sin,
You'll be a new creation.
Back to the beginning, back to the start,
He will renew your spirit and renew your heart.
So many times, so many places,
But you've finally realized who holds all the aces.
For you: a running race that He's been tracing.
Whatever you're facing, He will hold you together.

If you wait on Him, He will lift you up with might,
Upon your wings to fly like an eagle
And be redeemed through His Son.

'NO MORE STEPHEN'

Stephen Colbert is now off the air,
What seems like political could be quite radical.
CBS couldn't stress how the mess,
No less, no more, wasn't a score.
Simple maths and equations
For this money-losing station.
It's fascism at its finest, as a radio show incited.
It's not the ratings or the money,
It's the Trump-hating, which is not funny.
Stephen Colbert: a comedic voice,
A political choice for the leftist agenda.
A vendor of guests who come with their crests,
With feelings in their chests,
Pent-up emotions and TDS notions,
And all that's discussed reflects,
Attitudes and commotions.
Another year to wait,
March the end date.
A clean slate for CBS,
For Stephen, the last address.

'RON DE MANTIS'

Governor Ron DeSantis,
Is like a praying Mantis,
Cool, calm, and collected,
That's why so many have defected.
They want to be a part of the state that never departs,
From liberty, freedom, and choice.
He has never changed his voice.
Locked down and full of crime,
The other cities started to chime.
But when others tried to render,
He stayed true on his definition of gender.
Ron DeSantis, like a Mantis Ray,
His shadow has become a power play.
He never relents from his integrity,
His values he shows through his family.
What is next for the Alligator Governor?
The Whitehouse may be his next tenure.

'HUNTERS AND COLLECTORS'

Hunter Biden is not hiding the mistrust for his dad's
support,
His disgust, an F-bomb report.
The retort was incredible,
Sometimes it seemed illegible.
Is he back on the crack that he got from Barack,
Who's copping some flack?
What an interview of inception from the smartest Biden
sceptre,
A renowned artist who's part of the A-list.
Million-dollar paintings from the business entrepreneur,
An instituted cure for the Dems' demure.
Pure magic from the tragic Dems.
What a way to counteract the exact tact of the Republicans.
What foresight, what cunning to get the Dems running,
A stunning emergence, convergence of intelligence,
To put another Biden back in power, to shower us with
awesomeness and progressiveness.
The future looks bright with Hunter, he's back in the
limelight.
What a leader, he's out of sight.
So don't worry, don't despair,
With Hunter in charge, Republicans beware.

'ZOHAR MANDAMI, CAN HE, OR CAN'T HE?'

With his rapping persona on the table, are you gonna put
him in power?
Is this his hour for triumph, for victory?
Are you sure about his story?
Does it matter that he backtracks, even changes his
position?
The better likely candidate, can socialism commission a
better decision?
Can it support and distribute to make the state like the
statue,
The Lady of Liberty, who stands tall in adversity,
A symbolism of democracy and unity?
Remember the past as a point to make things last.
It's not just about redistribution or the Constitution,
The people are always the most important.
The one constant factor that should always remain,
The most important asset is the people, the people, the
people.
The governor selection will change the direction and
connection of the people.
What's good and what's best is always the test,
Of any true leader who becomes the succeeder of any
election.
Time will tell if what he sold, of promises told,
Will unfold a success story for people and for country,
In this place that is steeped in very proud history.

'TIRED OF FIGHTING'

Too tired to battle, too tired to speak.
Lord, I need you, I need your reach.
I've forgotten your Spirit, I've forgotten your grace,
My heart is hardened, please help me today.
When I come in or when I go out,
You watch me from afar, you know what I'm about.
Your level of mercy, your level of love,
Keeps me going through those times that are tough.
You pursue me with passion, you are zealous for my all.
Even though I fall, you look through the lens of your Son,
Jesus Christ.
Through my sins and my doubts, you are there throughout.
Through your Son, you see me clean without.
His robe you place on me, clean again.
You carry me, you love me, and hold me,
Never to leave nor forsake.
You give me the peace and rest I cannot fake.
Oh Lord, let me live all of my life in your presence,
To prove you are worthy, to be part of your remnant.
I am nothing without you, I will always say,
"Come, Lord Jesus, come today."

'MICHAEL KNOWLES BOWLS A BOUNCER'

Michael Knowles bowls the rhetoric with effective,
corrective statements.
Ready to debate and discuss with no fuss,
It's a must to listen to, as they continue to line up in a
queue,
To question your view on politics, gender, and race,
Straight to their face like a spray of mace.
Thoughtful and direct, willing to correct,
Their view that can be disputed,
Their diluted dilemmas which cause vile tremors.
Their thoughts and intentions are contentions for
discernment.
There's no pretending, they are not defending
Anything that makes logical sense.
Let's recompense that offence through your tact, your
presence.
Another voice for the right, to shed the light,
That you've been given for the times we are living.
Continue to strive and drive to survive,
Never leave your position of sight.
Michael Knowles, you're poles apart,
From those who start to impose those wild accusations.
So continue the vaccination,
A continued proclamation of everything that is right in this
world.

'BEN SHAPIRO MY HERO'

Ben Shapiro, my very first hero in conservative politics and
discussion.
Always much to say on where the left has decay, on things
that have no relevant data.
Their agenda is a blender that leaves you bewildered, but
always you have a response.
You listen to the questions, then center your arguments
around what you believe to be true.
The formulated facts that you exact with tact seem difficult
for their comprehension.
This, of course, is unfortunate for them.
Their distorted narrative is a disparative lens, and very
subjective right to the end,
But easily negated with your articulated vocation,
A narration of quick wit and speech.
We see eye to eye on so many issues, I thought nothing
could separate our views.
But alas, no less and no more is the Word,
Who became flesh and was heard,
Claiming that He was the Messiah.
He set my soul on fire, brought me out of the mire,
And now I speak to inspire, to bring Him the glory.
There is only one way, one truth, and one life.
It is Him who is worthy, Jesus the Christ.
This is not a compromise, I respect your standing.
I listen to your words; they are quite commanding.
But I will never exchange my commitment to Christ.
He was there at the beginning, and He rules my life.

'WHAT IS A WOMAN?'

Is that a troll, Matt Walsh?
Are you trying to extol or personify,
A reality that's not genuine in all its entirety?
With the professors and doctors you interviewed,
With discussion to find their definition on such a position,
This, of course, was amusing and bemusing as well.
What is a woman? Who can tell? It's subjective, a social
construct, you know.
But you were straight-faced throughout, of which I doubt I
could ever have remained.
But truly a masterclass, as an attack on the definition,
reconstitution on human classification, was made.
I laughed at the answers, so strong in their beliefs:
"Genders constructed; it's sex that is set in concrete."
You started the conversation where leaders from nations
struggled to exact a response.
It's so broad, so descriptive, it's also encrypted with
feelings of emotional nuances.
What you revealed was startling. Who thought it would be
global?
An international phenomenon that caught on so quickly,
Who would have thought there was so much ambiguity?

'DOUGLAS MURRAY, LIKE A HOT SAUCE CURRY'

A defender of Israel, God's chosen people.
Salvation for the Gentiles was given that day,
When Stephen was stoned and the Jews said, "No way!"
But a remnant remained, because God has it that way.
The seed war from the beginning is here because of
sinning.
Don't think He's not near, perfect love casts out all fear.
On the debate stage, with their berated rage,
He calmly destroys all the illogical ploys.
Douglas's motives, clearly articulated, not speculated
directives.
A travelled experience, lived-in existence,
A persistent seeker for truth, morals, and the West's way.
For a lot of countries, it's given them their best way.
Not everything is perfect, but it still has been worth it.
The past isn't the future, but it has its own culture.
This gives people a right to choose, but freedoms aren't
medians.
Some countries want to impose,
That what you post and say is in line with their woes.
So, Douglas, keep fighting, keep swiping them left,
After all, like you say: "The West has been best."

'FREE SPEECH IS OUT OF REACH'

Is free speech out of reach? Does hate speech try to teach,
That, as humans, our hearts are dark? There's a stark
difference between what is and what is not.
The reason is we're sinful; there's only one that exposes
that mark.
He is the great I am, who is the only one who can set a
moral objective.
That deceased this directive, a selective process that only
the Son, has exposed and deposed, because he chose to lose
his throne.
For you, he will condone; he will not leave you alone.
He will make the path clear if you give him your ear.
He will steer you there, where?
To the place of utmost fulfilment, peace beyond
contentment,
But a commitment is required; your free will is desired.
A jealous God, the host of the universe,
Who has created everything and every time for a purpose.
You are not alone in this world, he waits for your notice,
Your intent, your motive, to see what your response is.
Your free speech and your thoughts, your actions and
emotions.
You wonder why you're so empty, still searching for
answers.
There is only one divine, true commander.

'GERRYMANDERING IS PANDERING'

Gerrymandering is pandering and meandering.
Who suffers? The voters, to this sugar-coated attack.
They did it first, we'll do it back. What does it prove?
Nothing but a stat.
Because it's tit for tat on the Gerry Mander show, where it
stops, no one knows.
Both parties guilty to stack things in their favour,
Both parties knowing this is a flavour to savour.
When you're up and in control, take advantage, be that
bold.
When the tide turns and the tables are shifted,
This will all be sifted like wheat and flour to devour the
minority.
For the party who has less, that's how this was driven to
create this political mess.
Oh, what stress for the average person trying to navigate
these coercions, diversions, and perversions.
To create a majority, to stay in control, not down a fox hole
Or rabbit hole, because we'll be in control.
Who is it? The one that won the polls and,
Is now on a roll, Dems, do not fold.
A reset is needed, you have now been heeded,
A change of direction for your party, your people, and
leaders.
It's now or never, no time to waste, it's not too late.
Cut a new slate to negate this state.
Stop blaming the game, stay ahead of the train.
If not, you'll get railroaded and be stuck with a migraine.

'OUTSIDE OF TIME'

What is time, the concept sublime that sits in our mind?
You have so much more in store, ignore the seconds,
minutes,
And hours, daylight to darkness, the sunshine, the showers.
It moves silently with or without us. Why are we
concerned? Because our hearts yearn eternity.
It was there at the beginning, the reason we worry is
because of the sinning.
We were made immortal, we needed no other portal,
No other intangible way that we could stay and live
forever.
The knowledge we have of time eternal comes from the
Maker, who never made it this way.
The original decision to become our own gods has
shortened our life span and narrowed our thoughts.
Time, we don't have time, we don't own it.
It's a futile concept to place us in a zone.
Always wishing and wanting more, that's how the god of
this world controls your thoughts.
The one who created it stands outside of it,
Is the only one that gives you the peace of mind to make
that shift.
This world is temporary, it matters what we do.
Just as grass grows and withers, our life does too.
When you realise what you see is temporary, it's the
unseen that's arbitrary.
Your time becomes different, your time becomes a
sanctuary.
To the one above, who shows mercy and love,

Whose mercy is boundless and grace is above.
He sits, and He awaits, unaffected by time,
Your choice through Jesus, the way, the truth, and the life.

'JENNINGS SENDS A MESSAGE'

Scott Jennings is sending a message, the message is clear,
Bend your ear so you can hear,
That fear is not associated with his articulated answers.
His descriptions and discussions, even on Russia gate,
He doesn't propagate or inflate what's at stake.
Cool, calm, and collected, as he's dissecting the rhetoric,
The TDS agenda that the other guests render.
It's an intriguing discussion with what they are hustling,
But emotional detachment is a skill that you've learnt,
You've earnt my respect on quite a few levels,
The devil's in the detail which you provide often,
which doesn't bode well for the others who are scoffing.
It's an easy watch when you dismantle these panels and
handle the angles that these conversations take.
It's not fake news, but you're the reason I tune in to watch,
Brings a chortle from deep within.

'WORLD ON FIRE'

Step into the fire, where a cultural choir of poetic, political
satire collide and remain.
It will sustain your attention, a contention of thoughts and
ideas.
Praises and prayers collect under this umbrella from this
down under fella.
It demands your attention, it provokes your intentions.
It shifts dials on your smiles, with emotions to match.
It asks simple questions and states simple narratives, not to
be combative or disparitive,
But an examination is required of your inner person.
A coercion, a collection, not a misdirection.
The truth, as it stands, is simple in theory.
It's not a fairy, it gets hairy when your emotions are seared,
fuelled, and ignited.
But a dilemma evolves because of what unfolds.
Provoking your attention is what this book molds.

'KARMA WHAT IS IT'

What is Karma? Is it people getting what they deserve?
Does it represent drama?
Karma is coming for you, but who controls it?
Who says what is and what isn't?
Who is this make-believe God that you believe controls the
fortunes from times of old?
Who watches the checks and balances that weighs up your
motives and actions?
Is Karma a God, or an idol, or a spirit?
Do you believe the truth when you hear it?
Does this ease your unforgiveness?
Do you laugh at their misfortune?
They'll get what they deserve, what a nerve,
Don't curve my reaction, I'm justified, I need satisfaction.
How long will you wait? Who can tell?
This captivating spirit puts you in a cell, entrapped like a
prisoner.
It even makes you busier, believing all the time,
The way they wronged you was a crime.
Don't lock yourself up, don't lock yourself in,
All these emotions and thoughts are a sin.
Forgive like He does, or suffer the enactment,
The impactment of this fraction.
It'll split you in all directions and dissect your actions,
because it's a curse, eventually ending in a car carrying a
hearse.
There is no depending, this is a promise of God: if you
don't forgive, neither will I.

'DR. JOHN LENNOX LEWIS'

Dr. John Lennox Lewis, a maths Christian boxer exclusive,
An elusive mind that Jesus entwines.
Many debates, many discussions,
But he never deters from who he built his trust on.
He knows who's the truth, the root Word from the
beginning,
The great I Am who has solved all the sinning.
The salvation, the repentance, built on dependence,
Lennox firsthand has experienced this man.
This personal Saviour has curbed his behaviour,
Has set him apart, and now he doesn't waver.
From his purpose, his will,
Lennox remains still in His presence, His essence.
Has resonance, and his countenance rests upon his hands.
His ability to comprehend the things which confound the
average mind,
Comes from the inside, God's Spirit enables him,
To walk in servility, humility, credibility from all sides.
They can't deny his thoughts, and rebuttals scuttle their
stutters.
His ways and thoughts are higher than ours,
That's why Dr. Lewis debates, he knows what Jesus has
done for him,
He can do for you as well.

'MR SCHIFFS'IN A TIFF'

Adam Schiff, what a whiff of a tiff that you've created,
The pusher, the peddler, the Russia-gate meddler.
Who tried to propagate, and now in a mortgage debate,
A discussion on the rise for possibly telling lies
On owner representation, what a narration, what
insinuation.
"Nothing to see here, please move along,
Trump is the one who's doing all the wrong."
He made all the promises he just can't keep,
Regardless, the facts and the stats, they're so cheap.
We are all about emotions and feelings these days,
We know what we know about Republican ways.
Well, Mr. Schiff, there's a whiff of arrogance,
We'll sift that narrow glance, a comb through, no doubt,
To really find out.
If there's only truth and nothing else,
They'll investigate the claims and turn things around.
What was voiced so loud and clear,
Now seems to fall on deaf ears.
Nearly ten years of suffering, the truth has been buffering,
No more muffling, enough shuffling the cards so they stack
in your favour.
Nothing can change what you signed on that paper,
Primary residence or residence of convenience.
Until the court hearing, it's conjecture and hearsay.
Who knows what will happen, and if your pardon takes
sway.

'REST IN THE STORM'

The storms of this life are loaded with strife,
The winds are boisterous to doubt our minds.
When Jesus says, "Come, fix your eyes that way,"
The peace that He gives will give you rest today.

'THE REAL EXODUS'

Look at the chariots, look at the wheels.
The things in the sea, how did they get there for real?
Is it a fable, a myth, a mistake?
Did Gods' people really leave Egypt that day?
Did the blood on the door posts stop the Angel of Death?
Oh, please don't make up stories, it's far too inept.
The real depth of history is not this one for sure.
Too many movies, I don't believe there's any more.
And wandering the desert for 40 years on one pair of
shoes?
Please stop lying while I take a snooze.
Who cares if 3 generations are unaccounted for?
The Egyptians lost nothing, that's what hieroglyphics
record.
The altars at Mount Sinai, anybody could have made
The inscriptions and pictures, as a matter of fact,
Exodus ba-humbug, try another tact.
Not falling for this hack.
Show me some real proof and I might change my pact.
Not going back nor forward, no way,
None of this stuff impacts me today.
If God was all-knowing, the great I Am,
Why does He stand there and watch, never doing what He
can?

'THE STRUGGLE IS REAL'

Why do we struggle so much in this world?
The knowledge of good and evil,
Causes an upheaval, where all we want to do is worship
ourselves.
Our hearts are dark, our minds are feeble.
What is the answer, and who do we trust?
The only one who made us from dust.

'WE ARE SPIRIT WRAPPED IN FLESH'

We are spirit wrapped in flesh,
From the very first moment God gave us breath.
He breathed life into the dust, our body, our flesh,
Brought alive by the spirit, no less.
Our spirit is alive, but only made new,
When we consciously decide to repent and believe.
Sanctified through the water and spirit,
But the work of a lifetime is what our character needs.
How long or short the time that we have,
The only important thing is we know that He saves us.
Our flesh regenerated by the connecting of His spirit,
Returning to the original state that we were made.
But the knowledge of good and evil cause an upheaval;
The burden to carry our own cross
Is too hard for people that's why they remain lost.
But the light that makes you right is there by your side.
All of the time, He tries to shine,
But the darkness of our hearts makes us blind.
What we think we need is not what the hope is the faith in
Jesus indeed.
Please don't turn away, He calls you today,
He will make you right, His spirit will stay.
Through the wrongs, trials, and errors, He will never leave
you.
The cross, the example of His commitment,
Our burdens to bear, our sin He has omitted.
In your place He stands,
The scarred marks in His hands.

Forever your replacement, forever the plan,
Your redemption, your reconnection, there's nothing worth
more.
Salvation for you, He waits at the door.

'WHY THE SUFFERING'

Why the suffering, why the shame,
Why does it exist and who is to blame?
With everybody asking, it seems that God has been tasked
with this burden.
But when you start learning, this cursing from the
beginning,
Because of sinning, has placed this burden upon us.
This physical condition can only be alleviated on a spiritual
plain,
Otherwise we could go insane with this circular thinking,
Sinking our hope and our faith.
We have been called for a purpose, and until you know
Him you will create.
You will think, this is your way, this is your world, this is
your day.
This selfishness in thought reduces His spirit to nought.
He's alive in you, don't you know?
You are not singular, you're part of a family,
The one created before this disharmony,
This disconnection, this spiritual selection.
You are not alone, you never have been,
He's walked by your side, awaiting detection.
The way through this physical world,
Is the spiritual acceptance from the threefold,
The Trinity that has existed beyond infinity.
The world will soon be judged, the just and unjust.
The only way to escape, the only must:
Through Jesus alone, who has set in stone
The only way, the Truth, the Life,
To relieve you from your strife.

A double-edged sword that makes you right,
Pierced for our transgression, scarred for our needs,
Now you need to believe.
The spiritual way will set you free,
From your pain, it is the stain that remains.
The cause of suffering is sin, and this is its name.
Don't be flippant or coy, your soul it will take.
Who is your desire, who will you give your life?
You have only one chance, one time to get it right.
So don't waste, don't delay, don't wait,
Salvation for you is today.

'IMMIGRATION CITATION'

Immigration, what a depiction of moral connection,
A dejection of what is good, not gangs in the hood.
Gangstas first, and criminals too,
But let's wait for them in the homeland cue.
Does it feel like overreach?
What does this teach us?
They're illegal, you say, they can't overstay,
We will not pay.
But the proper channels weren't entrusted,
It's all turned to custard.
There's a fine line where morality encroaches,
As the law approaches.
It's definitely not one size fits all,
We are all immigrants, short and tall.
If we are talking about process,
Then I pray they get their due.
Because what will ensue is a cue,
For improper feuds of different colours and hues.
Everyone needs border control,
This is what Trump ran on.
I just pray for due process, not to get rained on,
Stained and drained by the inception of immigrant
dejection.

'AS A MANA OF FAITH'

Your faith rains manna from Heaven,
Unlike the leaven that sin only brings.
This spiritual food comes in different things,
In testing, in blessings, in trials, in confessing.
The faith of your mana is not near or far,
It's based upon Jesus, the tar on the ark.
The covering, the connecting that keeps us afloat,
Don't be deceived by the physical things you pursue.
All is vanity, it's about Jesus and you.
The spiritual food that encapsulates our flesh,
That moves us forward when we're in distress,
A mess, no less.
That Jesus cleans up, He continuously knocks,
Upon your mind and your door.
The leaven of sin is always trying to get in,
But the faith of the mana will always win.
In different degrees and circumstance,
His will is for the remnant.
Don't be deceived, believe in the spiritual mana,
That falls from the Father.
Gather what you need,
But don't concede, you're freed.
Take it from His ground,
And share it around.

'THE TREE OF GOOD AND EVIL'

Why the tree of good and evil, why on earth was it here?
It caused so much upheaval, it seems so unfair.
It effected our senses and now we're in chaos,
Immense, intense nonsense.
The choice we made and make every day,
Is the knowledge that we are gods, we control our physical
plane.
Deception, misconception, based on a false predication,
The deceit we accepted continues unobjected.
Takes root in our heart, which stays infected.
Yes, but why us, why this place?
We didn't choose this way.
We suffer the same wiles, guile from the enemy.
The choice is ours, free will must prevail.
Sin is here, it effects far and near,
Nothing but the blood can clean us from here.
To earth He came because we chose the sin game.
There is no winners for sinners,
It hinders our lives and makes us ashamed.
It stops the protection from the Creator above,
The one who gave His Son for us offers it in love.
He came because we lost, He calls you today,
Look to the cross.
One day that knowledge will be bound and wiped away,
Forever, never again to enter our life.
Connected again, we'll never be severed or tethered,
Complete in the one who is ever our leverage.
Who alone can handle the knowledge we can't,
He's always just in action, grace never far,
From you and your sanctification.

Soon the elements will vanish,
Like sin forever be banished.
The tree no longer a memory,
The earth and heavens reset to their glory.
Forever the holes a history, no longer a mystery,
Eternity with the river of life.
No more strife,
Living always in the light.

'THE REFINERS FIRE IS HERE'

The refiner's fire is upon you,
To inspire a transformation, a proclamation,
A new citation through the only promise that never fails,
That hails and sails above this world,
And transcends to a different level.
A spiritual plain that the devil tries to attain,
But only one remains constant.
A still, quiet voice,
Beyond the reproach, beyond the noise,
Beyond the system Jesus brings poise, control, and peace.
He says, "Be still," He holds you in His reach.
For those He loves, chastised and rebuked,
Look up to the heavens.
He stands to refute the lies and deceit beyond what we see,
Faith is believing, it's beyond the intrigue.
The refiner's fire is upon you,
Through the state that we are in,
Through the sin that dims the Revelation.
Your eyes are dim, your heart needs transformation.
Salvation is here today, there's no time to delay.
Don't stay in your rot, be transformed, I say,
By the light, His ray.
A new creation by His Spirit,
Becoming one with the Father and one with the Son.
His peace transcends, but your faith it depends.
It be-stills your heart,
It's time to start.

'JD IS ADVANCING HIS DANCING'

JD Vance, just dance, what a lance to his circumstance.
Newsome, a hue some of burdensome leadership,
Is meagre at best, trying to test Vance's resolve,
Trying to troll his involvement in the moulding,
emboldening of conservative views.
Gavin spews with no clues, just a simple rouse,
A creation at best of a futile troll, to test, to provoke a
reaction.
An action of distraction from the issues,
That he has effected, directed, infected, selected to ignore.
But your record implores a response, Gavin.
JD is advancing, his stancing, he's lancing, not glancing,
There's no second chancing.
So, Gavin, your attempt too thwart,
The run of the Vice President is done.
Trying to gain traction for attacking his actions,
Is laughable at best,
And he will pass the test.

'A TRIBUTE TO CHARLIE CAPTAIN KRIK'

Charlie, Captain Kirk, your work,
A concert of creative discussion, a repercussion,
A concussion of lived experiences with a teachable spirit.
Anointed by God for a ministry that put you in it,
Nowhere to hide, no time to delay.
A voice of a generation for a nation in degradation,
A compilation of institution, destitution.
A patriot, a seeker of truth,
A reliable source of a light that grew,
That ensued the next warriors of faith.
Your life ended by some ill-gotten fate.
Today, a turning point for the group you founded,
Where you sounded the alarm,
About the harm of choosing not life, not right, not the light.
On resurrection day, when Jesus calls your name,
When you stand with the multitude,
And your robe of righteousness upon you is laid,
"Well done, my good and faithful servant,
Now come and enjoy what I have made."

'CHARLIE LION HEART KRIK'

Charlie Kirk, lion heart,
God had your mission to impart.
A ministry of location, a devotion, vocation, the
destination,
The campuses to reach, the youth you needed to teach.
The truth with your light, you continued to fight,
Shine the way with your light and the Comforter.
A distorter you never contorted or imported unknown facts.
Your stats made cracks and holes to match,
Breaking down with reasoning and thinking.
From your mission, you never waned or were found
shrinking.
You are the reason they chose the Trump way.
They said it was impossible, but you didn't delay.
With dialogue and an infusion of passion, compassion,
A bastion of knowledge and understanding, commanding
and demanding responses.
You understood where you were needed,
And the warnings never impeded.
A voice, a roar to the nation,
A leader beyond elation.
The youth you connected, dissected, corrected.
Your roar heard loud and clear,
You were King of that jungle, no fear.
To stare down misinformation,
To break down the miscommunication,
You stood tall far above the rest.
Your testaments and accomplishments stood the test.
Your pride, your family, your devotion,
The truth, your deadly potion.

Now you will rest in Jesus.
God has secured your crest.
Your armour of flaming resilience,
A persistence of resistance was insistent.
The next roar will rise in your place.
God will never be in disgrace,
Never mocked, never shamed, never replaced.
Charlie, lion heart, has finished his race.

'BECOMING LIKE GOD'

We are gods in our own right,
What we worship brings our plight.
We contrive, we derive, we conspire,
We arrive at a destination where we create our own
explanation.
An incantation for our predication on how our lives should
be.
This, however, masks our connection to the only one
selection,
To be in the right direction.
Worshipping ourselves, how, may you say?
By justifying decisions with our own selfish way.
We make everything about us,
About what we want and why we should have it.
We were made for worship, so to ourselves we will plan it.
Everything comes back to me,
Regardless of how I perceive it to be.
I dictate, I control, I am at the center, I own my soul.
Free will has its demands, free will demands its freedoms.
Free will is love undoctored,
Free will from the one who completes us.
Forever He is seated at the right hand,
He is Jesus, He sees us and knows us by name.
We are the reason He came, to break your chains and your
shame.
Come, He beckons you today.

www.ingramcontent.com/pod-product-compliance
Lightning Source LLC
Chambersburg PA
CBHW060631130626
46555CB00002B/752